THE GENTLEMAN'S PLAYBOOK

to not being an a**hole

TYLER STAHLNECKER

The Gentleman's Playbook: To Not Being an Asshole Copyright © 2025 by Humor with Heart LLC

All rights reserved.

No part of this book may be reproduced in any form or by any electronic or mechanical means, including information storage and retrieval systems, without written permission from the author, except for the use of brief quotations in a book review.

Reader and/or Listener Warning

This book will probably offend everyone at least once.

If you've got a strong constitution for clean language or zero tolerance for anything even slightly inappropriate—please close this now and forever hold your piece.

Fair warning—if you don't mind strong language, some of this might sting a little. That's kind of the point, but I'd rather give you a heads-up than pretend it won't.

ISBN: 979-8-9938450-1-2

Interior design by Dawn Black
Cover design by Stefan Prodanovic

TABLE OF CONTENT

Introduction   5

Chapter 1:	Here's Why It's Complicated	16
Chapter 2:	The Mirror Test	24
Chapter 3:	How You May See, "Regular People"	34
Chapter 4:	You Around Different People	46
Chapter 5:	A Possible Asshole Painkiller	52
Chapter 6:	You Are What You Consume	58
Chapter 7:	The Two Types You Need to Read	68
Chapter 8:	Some of You Just Don't See It	76
Chapter 9:	This Shit Matters	92
Chapter 10:	Nobody's Perfect	108

INTRODUCTION

Someone either handed you this book or prayed that you'd find it.

You're probably confused right now. Maybe even just said, "What the fuck is this?"

Take a deep breath. You've just been called an Asshole.

Their public or private accusation probably just gave your little ego a good sack-tap. And your brain is already firing off, "How was I being the asshole?"

Perfect!

You're holding the right book.

Yeah, there are already books about assholes—how to spot them, survive them, avoid them, or rat them out. But let's be honest: that all sounds like classic bitch-ass avoidance behavior. This book's not about dodging assholes. It's about confronting the real issue—your asshole behavior.

So What Is an Asshole, Exactly?

Good question. For the sake of this book, here's my working definition:

An asshole is a man or woman who consistently makes everything harder for no fucking reason or worse; their own selfish reasons.

Statistically speaking by the time, you could shave your nut-sack or velvet snack pack, someone had already slapped that label on you.

I'm willing to bet in your life, at every job, team event, or family gathering you've always felt like the misunderstood one surrounded by soft, passive-aggressive, crybaby, pussies. Either way, this book's here to help you figure out what's really going on.

So, why should you read this book?

Because I'm not an expert. Just a guy with a healthy obsession for human behavior, a love for making people laugh, and—I've committed my fair share of assholery. Enough to cost me a few friendships, a couple relationships, disgustingly over-paid on a brand-new car, and no shit—$2,000 in a type of pyramid scheme. Like I said, just by being an asshole.

If you're laughing at me, great! That's okay. It's very hard but everyone needs to learn how to laugh at life kicking you in your fucked up places with its fake and gay crocks. And yes! Me calling your crocks fake and gay was an asshole thing to say. See how easy being an asshole is?

My particular flavor of asshole (pun not intended. Gross) flares up when I fail in front of people and they laugh. I get hot. Adrenaline starts to pump and for a few wild seconds, I feel stronger than ever. I burn with spectacular one hundred percent fully justified righteousness—like I've earned the right to break a chair or scream at whatever or whoever is in front of me. That's not who I want to be, ever! That's my ego saying, "I didn't get what I wanted!" or, "I got something I didn't want!" That's my bloated self-image throwing a tantrum because it lost control of the situation.

Then after my melt-down I start cracking jokes, talking louder and faster basically doing whatever I can to patch up the version of me I thought everyone saw five minutes ago.

Now, add a few drinks to that mix and I become like "that guy". The drunk friend at an MMA fight yelling, "Grab his dick and twist it!"

Remember that clip? "Twist that dick! The ooooooooold dick twist!"

Hilarious. If you know what I'm talking about and knew what to do with your hands, you and I are already friends.

Over a whole lot of time and focused practice—stuff like ball of light training (making your soul focus a ball of light and moving it through different parts of yourself) and yes, boring-ass breath work.

I've started noticing the little warnings—my face getting hot, knee bouncing, breath racing, jaw clenching over something that, let's be honest, doesn't even matter. A job? A game? Some random bitch-ass on the freeway? None of that's worth handing over my peace of mind. If my ego crumbles every time I feel an L or feel judged, I'm not building character—I'm just role-playing as a mature adult instead of being one.

Having a little more humility now, a clearer sense of my priorities, and just enough perspective to maybe help someone else sidestep a few of the social landmines I face-planted into.

After giving it some thought over the last few weeks—and I'm starting to believe being an asshole isn't some permanent stamp on your soul.

Despite whatever reaction just fired off in your head calling bullshit on me, hear me out. I'm convinced it's not who you are—it's what you do.

You can be a perfectly normal person and do an asshole thing.

You could be a psychopath… and not act like an asshole.

You might be bipolar, anxious, exhausted, socially awkward, neurodivergent, or just deeply misunderstood—and still not be one.

Because "asshole" doesn't describe who you are deep down.

It describes the smelly, messy, socially unpleasant thing you dumped on someone.

That moment. That attitude. That tone. That behavior. Make sense?

Being in my mid-thirties, I'm starting to realize most asshole behavior isn't part of some grand evil plan. It's usually a mix of bad habits, misdirected instincts, and weak or warped values.

You'd be surprised how easy it is to pick up this kind of crap—just from stress, bad role models, or never being called out on how you treat people. Hell, sometimes you are called out… you just don't listen. Trust me, it catches up. Always does.

One day, people stop laughing at your jokes, stop inviting you places, stop answering. And you realize—damn, I've been on my own for a while now.

I don't want that for you. It's happened to me, so I get it.

The good news? That means it can change. Learn to catch yourself. Choose a better response.

To my understanding typical asshole choices stem from,

- Ego over Empathy.
- Avoidance over Accountability.
- Insecurity over Connection.
- Blame over Ownership.
- Validation over, Growth.
- Sarcasm over Honesty.
- Judgment over Understanding.
- Certainty over Openness.
- Criticism over Contribution

The ways to be an asshole seem endless—too messy for me to sort out like some behavior bingo card. So I'm not aiming for clinical precision here.

Being one isn't a full-time gig—it's a pattern of choices or balled up emotions. And anyone can fall into the actions that gets the more sensitive individuals reaching for their asshole stamp to label you. Even if it is a "first offence" type situation.

Now, before you slam this book shut—this book isn't here to shame you. It's not about calling out people—it's about calling out behavior.

The patterns we slip into.
The ones others excuse—until they don't.
The ones that quietly push people away.

This isn't a hit list. It's a mirror. And the message is simple:

Stop being an asshole. Just… stop.

You're not helping anyone—not the people around you, and definitely not yourself.

This book is about getting to know yourself better figuring out where the asshole behavior can begin and end. It's about knowing when to shut up, show up, and step up. You'll laugh, you'll cringe, and if nothing else, at least you'll know what kind of asshole not to be.

It'll be harder than keeping your cool when you're right. But easier than cleaning up, after being wrong.

Now, let's get started!

CHAPTER 1:

HERE'S WHY IT'S COMPLICATED

> (Or: Why People Seem Cool with You
> One Minute—and Cold the Next)

You've probably had moments where people act like you're the best damn friend they've got. Like when you showed up hungover to help your buddy with a dead car battery, no questions asked. Total legend move. While holding the red and black cables you make a joke about jumping his mom's nipples to charge her wheelchair and get a good laugh.

But then… a week later, with all the dudes and their ladies you crack the same joke, and suddenly everyone's looking at you like you just pissed in the punch bowl.

What the hell happened?
They were chill a second ago. They laughed last time. Now they're all "too sensitive"?

That's a textbook case of not reading the room. Maybe the mom was within earshot, or maybe randomly bringing up old lady nipples probably sounded nasty or creepy as hell to the girls. And if the dudes laughed? Yeah, you know on the way home it's a 45-minute, one way conversation about your dumbass comment. And everything else they can pile on to not invite you to things. Including but not limited to:

- "I don't like the way he… (Insert one million damn reasons they have to pick from.)"

- "Did you hear him actually say— (She's got a whole history of you to quote from and toss on the fire)

- "I just don't understand people like that." (Her confusion implies the man has to now solve a problem that didn't exist before your dumb fucking comment.)

Either way, bad subject multiplied by worse timing.

Welcome to the complicated reality of being that guy—the guy people like... until they don't. The guy people defend... until they can't.

Believe it or not, people want to like you. Most human beings don't keep their social settings stuck on "Fuck off." They want to make the good kind of memories—the moments you had their back, made them laugh, or bailed them out. That stuff matters. It builds goodwill.

But here's where it gets messy: goodwill runs out if every other interaction feels like an emotional CrossFit class.

Because you're not only the guy who helped a friend in crisis.
You're also the guy who drops roast-level insults at a funeral.
Or the girl who calls it "just being honest" when everyone else calls it "Rude."
You're the guy who can be loyal as hell... and also emotionally unavailable, sarcastic, and exhausting.

And yeah—people might still keep you around.
You're useful. You're funny. You've got history.
But they're also constantly calculating:

"Can I invite him to this thing?"
"Do I need to warn people first?"
"Is it worth it today?"

That's what makes this whole thing so damn complicated.
You do show up when it matters—sometimes.
But that doesn't cancel out all the moments when you're the social equivalent of 10 crying babies on a plane.

You might be wondering:

"If I'm such a problem, how come we always eventually end up talking anyways?"

Because connection is messy.
Because people crave someone who "gets them."
And sometimes, even assholes provide that—when they're not actively torching the vibe.

Maybe you're the guy who laughs at the same weird jokes. Who doesn't judge someone for falling apart. Who can talk about real stuff without making it awkward or funny.

That kind of connection is rare—and people hold onto it as long as they can.
But even the best connections have limits.
And if you keep pushing yours, one day you're going to realize everyone's laughing around you, not with you anymore.

Keep in mind this book isn't here to exile you.
It's not about turning you into a soft, sanitized version of yourself.

It's about giving you the social playbook no one handed you growing up.
Because chances are, no one ever taught you how to express yourself without detonating social landmines every ten minutes.

This is about helping you stay funny, loyal, and real—without being the human version of a warning label.

Here's the truth:

Most people don't want you gone.
They just want to stop flinching when you speak. They want to invite you without a back-up plan.
They want you to get it—not change who you are, simply turn some dials down so you stop burning bridges and calling it warmth.

Everyone's got an inner asshole.
The win is learning how to manage yours before it manages you.

Because yeah, life's already chaotic enough. You being a decent human with higher-than-normal social awareness? That's rare. That's valuable. That's attractive.

So bring the heat—just stop setting the place on fire.

CHAPTER 2:

THE MIRROR TEST

> (Let's put a mirror directly in front of your awareness)

Let's start here—before the fresh fade, before the firm handshake, before the whiskey on the rocks, the weed pen in your pocket for match, or the late-night group chat full of fire emojis and half-baked life advice.

Who are you when it's dead quiet? When the notifications stop, the room is still, and no one is watching. What do you see in the mirror when it's just you, your reflection, and the weight of your own damn expectations?

Because that guy—that's the baseline you.

We all perform. We all have "on" and "off" versions of our selves. You've probably got the version that shows up to work, the one that shows up to a date, and the one that shows up to a group chat after a few drinks. But here's the uncomfortable question:

How far is your real self from the one you're pretending to be?

That gap—the space between who you are and who you want to be—that's your personal battleground. And the more honest you are about it, the better shot you've got at not being an asshole.

Who Are You, really?

Who are you when there's no role to play? No boss to impress. No group to fit in with. No performance?

That's the version people closest to you have to live with.

Being a gentleman isn't about having multiple masks that fit the room. It's about having one set of values that shows up consistently—even when it's inconvenient.

Here's a little science to sneak in behind your bourbon: Psychologists break personality into what they call the Big Five traits. Most people fall somewhere along each spectrum—and the cool part? You can shift a little over time, depending on who you are now and who you're trying to be.

Let's paint them in broad strokes for the average guy:

1. **Openness to Thoughts or Experiences**

   - Low: You prefer routines, don't like surprises, and keep things safe.

   - High: You're creative, curious, spontaneous. You've probably tried painting, skydiving, or kombucha—at least once.

2. **Conscientiousness**

   - Low: You're messy, forget plans, maybe lose track of time a lot.

- **High:** You're organized, disciplined, the kind of guy who actually folds his laundry on the same day he washes it.

3. **Extraversion**

    - **Low:** You like alone time. Small talk drains you.

    - **High:** You're the guy who charges up in a crowd. You work the room without even trying.

4. **Agreeableness**

    - **Low:** You'll tell someone their haircut sucks and call it "honesty."

    - **High:** You're a people-pleaser. You want everyone to feel included, even if it means biting your tongue.

5. **Neuroticism**

    - **Low:** You're even-keeled, chill, and tough to rattle.

- High: You overthink. You lose sleep over one weird comment from a stranger.

You're somewhere on each of these. Knowing where you fall doesn't define you—but it damn sure helps explain you. Self-awareness isn't about labels. It's about tools. Tools you can sharpen and use. I believe in no way are you stuck at any particular level, in any particular category—this is simply an awareness of your baselines. If you become more disciplined, you'll move—up or down—on one or more scales. That's the point: knowing where you are so you can choose where you grow.

If you're curious where you land, you can take a free Big Five personality test online—there are plenty of versions, and most only take about ten minutes. It's not some BuzzFeed quiz to tell you what kind of unicorn you are—it's a tool backed by a couple decades of research, countless experiments, and recognized by clinical psychiatrists. Knowing your scores can give you a clear view of your strengths—and where your inner jackass might be hiding.

Now! All the crap you've read so far is, more or less, you looking inwards. Hears how I've been able to best describe looking outwards.

Every person walks around wearing a pair of mental glasses behind their eyes. They're how your brain filters and frames what's coming in—turning raw information into meaning before you even know it.
Each pair represents what you value most at that moment—safety, pride, connection, control, attention, whatever.
Those values tint how you see the world. The wrong pair at the wrong time can turn small moments into massive misunderstandings.

You can stack them, scratch them, or let them get foggy over time. If you don't clean them—meaning, if you don't check in on what you actually value—they start to warp your view.

And once that happens, even the clearest truth looks a little distorted.

If you drop down the pride or control lenses, you'll start seeing rivals where there aren't any—every comment sounds like a challenge, every bump feels personal.

If you drop down the blame-and-validation lenses, you'll spend all your energy attempting to prove yourself right instead of improving your situation. You'll chase praise instead of accountability—and wonder why nothing changes.
Praise tells you what you want to hear; accountability is telling you what you need to hear.

The sting of being wrong hurts everyone. If you won't learn from it, then stop being such a pussy.

And to be clear—I'm not claiming to have discovered some ancient mystical psychological technique. This isn't groundbreaking. I'm just pointing out something everyone does but never notices.

And here's the wild part:
Most people don't even know they're wearing anything.
They think the color's they feel just fall out of the sky—not realizing they choose what glasses to put on and when to put them on.

You ever argue with your partner, and they somehow manage to play keep away from any point that gives you the advantage? Their simply switching glasses on you, mid conversation.

But once you notice you're wearing mental glasses, you can choose them—on purpose—instead of letting your emotional autopilot pick them for you.

For example:
You see a dad yelling at his kid in the store. Instantly, your "protect the child" glasses slide on—you tense up, ready to step in. Then the

"self-preservation" pair kicks in: Wait, if I jump in here, this could blow up fast. Maybe even legally. So you freeze, and the "judgment" glasses take over. What kind of asshole yells at his kid like that?

Then the kid—who turns out to be about fifteen—slams a boxed toy to the floor and starts full-on gorilla-pounding it like he's auditioning for a toddler reboot. Suddenly, your brain swaps again—oh, now you're wearing the "yep, I get it" glasses.

Gentleman Check:

Try to think of it this way.

Empathizing is simply matching lenses.
You don't have to agree—you just have to see through the same tint long enough to understand why they're wearing that combination of lenses.

These "glasses" quietly **color your reality**.

YOU, decide what you see.

CHAPTER 3:

HOW YOU MAY SEE, "REGULAR PEOPLE"

> (Or: Why Everyone Else Seems So Soft, Fake, or Confusing to You)

If you've ever thought,

- "Why is everyone so sensitive?"
- "What did I do this time?"
- "That joke killed with the boys earlier, what changed?"

And regular people? Yeah. They look like emotional wrecks playing charades with their social codes.

But here's the twist—maybe it's not them.

Maybe it's time to clean your lens.

Section 1: Emotional People Are Not Broken

To an asshole, emotion looks like weakness. Crying? Oversharing? Asking if you're okay when you're clearly not? What the hell is all that?

But here's the truth:

"Regular people" aren't broken for feeling things. You're just not fluent in their emotional language.

You act like a tourist talking shit at a local for not speaking English... when you're the one visiting.

Common Asshole Thoughts:

- "God, why are they so dramatic?"
- "They're crying again? Over what?"
- "This isn't a big deal."

Reality Check:

- Just because it's not a big deal to you doesn't mean it's not bleeding out for them.

- And unless asked, your unfiltered thoughts should stay right where they came from—wedged firmly up your own ass.

I get it—it's hard. Sometimes I'd rather butt-chug red Kool-Aid and throw myself through some drywall than sit through someone else's emotional spiral. But give it thirty to forty solid minutes.

(Pro tip: Set a mental timer. Acknowledge their feelings and explain why you understand or don't understand about why they feel that way, summarize what they said, then ease into something lighter—change the subject, suggest an activity, whatever works. You're not fixing their whole life. You're just showing them they're not in it alone.)

Section 2: Social Signals Are Real (Even If You Suck at Seeing Them)

You ever walk into a room and say something you thought was fine... and suddenly it's silent? Or you made a joke and now people are avoiding you like you're a fart in an elevator?

That wasn't a glitch in the Matrix. That was a social cue you missed.

Fix the Filter:

Before you launch your next joke, do a quick vibe check. Not a deep spiritual meditation—just… notice the room. Are people chuckling at dad jokes or swapping roast battle zingers?

Think of humor as a sliding scale:

Level 1 – "Dad Joke Territory" No cussing. No sex. No death. No dismemberment. No lawsuits. Stuff like:

"Did you know Chuck Norris can pull a wheely on a unicycle?"

Level 10 – "Kill Tony Free-for-All" Roasting. R-rated. Sharp insults flying like dodgeballs in prison.

"Your face looks like your parents argued during conception."

Now here's the thing: Most rooms aren't permanently locked at Level 1 or Level 10. They float. But if someone just told a knock-knock joke about bananas, maybe don't follow it up with a squirting joke.

That's not "matching energy"—that's showing up to a water balloon fight with a flamethrower.

So yeah. Read the room. Match the moment. And if you miss? Own it. Laugh with them. Adjust.

You're not banned from being funny. You're just learning to not be a human landmine.

Section 3: Regular People Don't "Need Constant Validation." They Just Don't Want To Be On Guard.

You might think regular people are "soft" because they want their opinions respected or their boundaries honored. You might see that as needy or over emotional.

That's because you were probably raised to think approval equals weakness and that vulnerability = a trap.

What You've Might of Though:

- "They need me to baby them."
- "They want a trophy for existing."
- "I say one thing and now I'm the bad guy?"

What's Actually Happening:

- People want to know they're not going to get ambushed, mocked, or steamrolled.

- It's not about ego—it's about safety.

- You don't have to be fake. You just have to stop acting like honesty means "cutting people down."

A Better Way:

- Try just listening—like, actually listening—not waiting for your turn to speak.

- Give a compliment without immediately tacking on a roast like it's some emotional bait-and-switch.

- Ask how they prefer feedback instead of lobbing a truth grenade into the conversation uninvited.

And if you actually value the relationship? Then honor their request—assuming you're not both just here to emotionally Supplex each other for sport.

Section 4: If You Think Everyone Else is the Problem…

This is the part where the mirror gets a little uncomfortable. If everyone you meet has a problem with your tone, your jokes, or your presence… it might not be a global conspiracy.

It might be you.

Signs You Might Be the Asshole:

- You call it "just being honest," but no one else seems to want your version of honesty.

- You think everyone's "too emotional," but they all seem happier than you.

- You say, "I don't do drama," but somehow, you're always surrounded by it.

Try This Instead:

- Start assuming other people aren't idiots—they're just operating on a system you never bothered to understand.

- Learn their rules. Not to fake it—but to stop stepping on social landmines every five minutes. Such as,

  - Giving "brutally honest" feedback no one asked for.

  - Laughing at your own joke… then explaining it… twice.

  - Saying "calm down" to someone who is very much not calm.

  - Simply thinking you can tell someone what to do. (Personal note: Holy shit this one pisses me off.) Who do you think you are asshole! Human to human have the decency to ask.

Final Thought:

You're not broken. You're just not listening. The world doesn't need you to be soft. But it does need you to stop confusing bluntness with bravery and detachment with strength.

If everyone seems hard to connect with, maybe it's time to drop the asshole lens and start seeing people for what they really are:

Messy, emotional, imperfect—but worth the effort. Kind of like you.

CHAPTER 4:

YOU AROUND DIFFERENT PEOPLE

> (Why You're Chill with Strangers but a Dick to Your Sister)

You ever notice how someone's super chill with their barista... but talks to their partner like they're a customer service rep who lost their luggage?

Or how someone's all smiles at work, a mess at parties, and a storm cloud at home?

That's not "having different sides." That's selective character.

Why You Act "Cool" with Strangers but Blow Up at Your Partner

Because strangers don't know your baggage. They don't know that your, 85% full of shit and 15% full of, other bullshit.

Strangers are easier to impress up front. Low risk. You can walk away at any moment with little to no consequences.

But your partner?

They know the real you — and your tricks. They see your patterns. And they're close enough to poke your ego, which makes them the easiest target when you're frustrated, insecure, or overwhelmed. Especially if they depend on you — because deep down, you know they're more likely to stay.

A lot of people save their best manners for strangers and their worst moods for the people they love most. That's not love. That's emotional laziness.

Work You vs. Party You vs. Real You

- Work You: Measured. Polished. Says "no worries" even when there's absolutely a worry.

- Party You: Loud. Looser. Possibly thinks karaoke is a flex.

- Real You: TBD.

How Ego Morphs Depending on Your Audience

Your ego's a shapeshifter.

Around people who intimidate you? It might shrink into silence.

Around people who admire you? It puffs up like a prize rooster in a mirror.

And around people who challenge you? It might bare its teeth and get nasty—fast.

The ego isn't evil.

It's your psychological hype-man.

It's the part of your brain that says, "You matter," even when some people in the world say, "You don't."

It wants to protect you, prove you, promote you… and sometimes, straight-up hijack you.

Neuroscience doesn't pin ego to one structure, but it does suggest it draws heavily from things like your default mode network, your social threat response, and your mirror neurons. These neurons fire when you see others act a certain way, and your ego uses that feedback loop to adjust your performance accordingly.

In short:

Your ego watches. Then it edits. Then it performs. And when your confidence is rooted in that performance—when it's reactive instead of solid—you become whatever the room demands. Your personality becomes a mood ring. If your energy constantly shifts depending on how much praise, power, or control you feel in the room…

You're adapting to survive. And survival mode is where a lot of unintentional assholery lives.

Gentleman Check:

Are you consistent—or just convenient?

Who you are around the people you don't have to impress... is who you really are. And if that guy isn't someone you'd want to date, hire, or high-five—good news.

You can still build him.

CHAPTER 5:

A POSSIBLE ASSHOLE PAINKILLER

(Not quite the antidote, but…)

If you want to dull the sting of social pain and rejection, you'll need to swallow a pill the size of a horse suppository—and that pill is called Situational Awareness.

Most people think situational awareness means scanning the room like some douchebag version of James Bond, In reality, the first step isn't the room—it's you. If you don't know your own mental and emotional state, you'll misread everything else around you.

3 Anchors for Self-Situational Awareness:

1. Check Your Body → Are your shoulders tense? Jaw locked? Breathing shallow? Your body often knows you're stressed before your brain admits it.

2. Check Your Focus → Ask, "What am I actually paying attention to right now?"

If you're locked inside your head replaying arguments or daydreaming, you're blind to the real room.

3. Check Your Impact → Quickly scan how others are reacting to you. Are they leaning in, pulling back, cutting eye contact, or mirroring you? Their micro-adjustments are mirrors to your presence.

The Trick: Build a 10-second loop. Every so often, do a fast scan—body, focus, impact. It keeps you grounded in yourself and tuned into the environment without overthinking.

Once you develop your self-awareness you'll begin to understand others and try seeing through someone else's windshield for a second. It's probably cracked (their trauma), dirty (Their bad habits), and the wipers are shot (No positive influences)—but hey, that's the point.

I'm willing to bet you probably didn't wake up thinking, "Today's the day I ruin lives!" They're reacting to their own mess—pain, stress, bad wiring, or years of built-up emotional junk they don't know how to clean out.

How to Trigger a Perspective Shift (a.k.a. Empathy Without Losing Your Edge):

1. Label Their Pain (Mentally, Not Out Loud)

- Before you fire back, try asking yourself:

- "What's this person actually carrying right now?" (-Tip, don't compare with what you're carrying.)

- Just putting a label on their emotional state—*"They're scared," "They feel overlooked," "They're insecure as hell"—*takes the sting out of their behavior and reminds you it's not about you.

2. Try on Their Shoes—Even If They're Ugly as Hell

- Imagine living their day, their responsibilities, their fears.

- You don't have to agree with them to understand them.

- And understanding, even just a little, makes you a better human by default.

3. Use the Magic Phrase: "I Wonder What Happened to Them…"

- Not "What's wrong with them?"—that's judgment.

- "I wonder what happened to them…" is curiosity. And curiosity leads to compassion.

Final Thought:

You don't have to fix everyone's problems. You just have to recognize that they exist. And that tiny mental shift? That's what separates the jackasses from the gentlemen.

CHAPTER 6:

YOU ARE WHAT YOU CONSUME

(Why You Might Be Acting Like the Wrong Kind of Main Character)

Let's start here:
You didn't choose most of your reactions.
You downloaded them.

I had a weirdly creative idea to explain better how you became you—in broad strokes:

Think of every experience like a bite of mental food.
Your brain chews it, breaks it down, and turns it into whatever emotional protein it needs.

Here's how that digestion goes down:

Raw Data (the bite):
You see, hear, or feel something. It's just information—flavorless, context-free, no meaning yet.

Awareness (the taste buds):
Your mind decides what's worth noticing. Not every flavor makes it past the tongue—some stuff just gets spit out instantly.

Filter (the stomach acid):
Now your brain mixes that info with your personal enzymes—your moods, your memories, your expectations. This is where the flavor changes.

Meaning (the absorption):
You pull nutrients out of the experience—the lesson, the emotion, the story your brain tells itself about what happened.

Emotion (the bloodstream):
The meaning gets pumped through your system. You feel it. That's the signal that tells your body, "This matters."

Belief (the tissue):
Over time, those emotional signals stick. They become muscle memory—beliefs, habits, reactions.

Identity (the whole body):
Keep repeating that loop and boom—you've built a whole self out of the experiences you've digested.
You are what you mentally eat.

Between the ages of four and fourteen, your brain was basically a **collection plate for drama**.

You took in whatever got passed around—cartoons, reality TV, video games, movies, your parents arguing about bills, your friend's older brother's "alpha" advice, YouTube screamers, even how your favorite characters handled stress or won arguments.

You didn't just watch it.
You absorbed it.
And over time, it shaped the **autopilot version of your personality**—the part of you that kicks in when you're flustered, defensive, or under pressure.

It's not your fault.

Your brain was just doing what brains do—**looking for patterns and copying what worked**. It didn't care if those patterns were emotionally mature, healthy, or even remotely useful. It just went:

"Ah. That's how people get respect.
That's how people get love.
That's how people stay safe."
Copy. Paste. Repeat.

You Selected Your Data Set Without Knowing

You didn't consciously build your personality. You inherited it through **osmosis, entertainment, and survival instinct**.

You might think you have free will—but let's be real.
If you've ever:

Ghosted someone because "conflict is awkward,"

Tried to "win" an argument using a zinger you heard from a movie,

Shut down emotionally because showing vulnerability felt gross, then congratulations: **your subconscious is still running code from 2004.**

And what we call a "personality trait"?
Might just be a **reflex you never updated**.

Default Settings Are Loudest Under Stress

When things go sideways, you don't usually show up as your best self.
You show up as your **oldest, loudest influence**.

That cocky character who always had the last word? He's got your mouth.

That distant, stoic hero who said nothing and punched walls? He's steering your emotional availability.

That dramatic TV meltdown moment that somehow looked badass? Yep. You're reenacting that in your group chat right now.

Your mind grabs whatever behavior once looked like control and throws it into the scene—even if it doesn't fit, even if it's not you, even if it gets you absolutely nowhere.

Emotional Spam Filters Are Built From Exposure

You think you're reacting to reality.
But a lot of times, you're reacting to **simulations** you watched a hundred times growing up.

Someone takes too long to text back? Your brain doesn't wait—it casts them as the villain and starts cueing emotional background music.

Your partner's quiet for a minute? You don't ask. You assume. Cheating. Leaving. Hiding something.

Why?
Because that's how the plot usually goes, right?

Your mammalian brain isn't always rational.
It's **narrative-driven**, and **trained on reruns**.

Imitation Confidence vs. Actual Control

When you're calm, maybe you're authentic.
But under pressure? You become your own glitchy deepfake.
You overcorrect. You impersonate. You panic-perform.

You try to be smooth like that movie guy.

Or clever like that comedian you grew up quoting.

Or dominant like that rage-podcast guru.

But you're not them.
And honestly? They probably weren't even that good at being themselves.

Pretending Comes With a Cost

When you mimic someone else:

You lose your edge.

You feel off.

You come across fake—because **you are**, in that moment.

Worst of all, you teach your brain to do it again next time.

Which means you're reinforcing a version of yourself that doesn't even feel right—and deep down? You know it.

The Real Power Move?

Hold your ground without losing yourself.

That's the flex.
Not the loudest voice in the room. Not the snarkiest comeback.
Just calm, present ownership of your own damn nervous system.

You can:

Be assertive without being an asshole

Be kind without being walked on

Be quiet and still command the room

That's not weak. That's controlled.
That's **not a rerun**. That's you.

Gentleman Check:

Are you reacting from experience—or re-running some half-scripted character you downloaded 20 years ago?

Update your code.
You don't need to delete your past.
But you do need to decide who's driving your reactions now.

CHAPTER 7:

THE TWO TYPES YOU NEED TO READ

> (This changed the game for me making that good first impression: when you meet someone, you really just need to match two things — their energy level and their emotional level.)

If someone's chill — calm, relaxed, speaking softly — match their energy plus one. Don't out-chill them, just let them know you can be chill. If they're loud, animated, talking with their hands? Match their energy minus one. Let 'em know you can ride the wave and you're not trying to one up them.

Then there's their emotional level. If they're high emotion, they'll be dramatic, expressive, and react hard. If they're low emotion, you'll feel like you're carrying the whole damn conversation.

That one's trickier, because emotional levels usually tie to something — or someone — they care about. So here's the rule: don't talk shit about the thing they love. Unless you're very funny. Like, very—very funny.

(Spoiler: you're probably fuckin' not.)

But if you can tune into those two things? You give yourself a real shot.

And no—I'm not telling you to fake it, pretend you like something you don't, or nod along like a golden retriever in a job interview. That's not the point. The point is relatability.

If you're naturally low-energy, even if you've got big emotions under the surface, you're probably not going to match someone who's bouncing off the walls. And that's okay — you're not supposed to.

This isn't about changing who you are. It's about showing people, especially when you first meet them or when they're going through something, that you actually give a shit. That you're tuned in.

And honestly? That's rare. So it stands out.

1. Emotional Sensitivity Setting
How strongly someone feels and reacts emotionally (to praise, criticism, social energy, tone, etc.)

- High sensitivity = takes things personally, reads between lines, deeply affected by mood/tone

- Low sensitivity = harder to read, emotionally steady or disconnected, doesn't react to subtle cues

2. Energy Output Setting
How much physical, mental, and social energy they naturally operate with day to day

- High energy = talks fast, fidgets, needs stimulation, intense

- Low energy = slow to act, calm, measured, takes time to process

Your Example:
You're high on both:

- High emotional sensitivity = You feel what people are feeling, you're probably empathetic but might overthink reactions or tone.

- High energy = You talk fast, joke fast, probably lead the room without trying.

That combination makes you magnetic and a little overwhelming to people who are low on either scale.

What This Means in Real Life

It explains so many "clashes" or awkward interactions:

- High energy, low sensitivity person can come off as steamrolling or tactless (even if they mean well).

- Low energy, high sensitivity people may seem quiet or shy but are hyper-aware of tone and intent—if you speak too loud or fast, they shut down.

- Low energy, low sensitivity types? Can seem cold, indifferent, "asshole-ish," but really might just not process social signals quickly.

- High energy, high sensitivity (like you)? Passionate, intense, warm... but risk being "too much" for chill types or "too emotional" for blunt types.

This mirrors a few real psychological models:

- The Big 5 Personality Traits
- Emotional Sensitivity overlaps with Neuroticism and Agreeableness
- Energy Setting overlaps with Extraversion and Openness
- Social Cue Processing

Studies show that people who are more emotionally reactive have stronger amygdala responses, while high-energy types often score higher on dopamine-driven traits (novelty seeking, spontaneity, reward-chasing).

CHAPTER 8:

SOME OF YOU JUST DON'T SEE IT

> (Intent doesn't buy you a free pass. Impact matters.)

Just because you don't mean to be an asshole doesn't mean you get to act like one and still expect the gold star treatment from everyone.

Some of you genuinely miss the cues—tone, timing, body language, those subtle emotional shifts, and/or subtext within a conversation. You're not trying to be rude... but major pile up is coming.

Even if you don't see it.

1. Emotionally Colorblind

You say the wrong thing at the wrong time with full confidence. You:

- Miss sarcasm
- Take everything literally or not serious enough

- Say "Their emotions are not my problem." when someone's hurting—not cruel, just weirdly flat

You're not evil. You're just operating without half the emotional color wheel. That blank expression you give when someone's trying to be vulnerable? Yeah, it's not as invisible as you think.

2. Socially Tone Deaf

You hear words—but completely miss how they were said. You:

- Bulldoze right through tension like a motivational speaker on cocaine
- Think "I'm fine" means "Cool, carry on!"
- Assume a polite smile means "go ahead," not "please stop"

You're not ignoring people—you're just missing the music behind their words. But that doesn't mean it's their job to shout.

Why This Matters in a Book That's Literally About You

Because this kind of behavior looks like asshole behavior from the outside. Even if you have good intent, people still feel hurt, ignored, or trampled. And if you want to stop being labeled "that guy," you need to start building some awareness.

What You Can Do (If This Sounds a Little Too Familiar):

- Ask people how you made them feel, not just what they think

- Try to find the core values they are trying to protect. Quick fact: Almost never going to match yours. Respect them anyways.

- Keep a socially sharp friend around and listen when they pull you aside

- Patience, patience, and more patience.

Gentleman Check: Are you giving people a chance to feel understood?

Not an Asshole—Just Clumsy as Hell

1. You interrupt constantly

You think you're just excited. You want to relate. You're yelling "Me too!" with your mouth before your brain gets a chance to say it better. But to them? You're steamrolling their moment.

2. You make jokes in serious moments

They're opening up. You crack a joke. To them? You just made light of something deeply painful. To you? That was survival mode. Humor is how you stay in the room when it's too real.

3. You over explain or hijack the conversation

They say one thing, and you give a TED Talk about how to fix their life. You're trying to be helpful—but it feels like you're flexing your wisdom while ignoring their need to vent. Advice is not always connection. Sometimes it's noise.

4. You get defensive when called out

They bring up something small. You freak out. Not because you're a villain—but because it hits a nerve. You already feel like you're failing, and now you're trying to outrun the feeling by snapping back. That's not growth—That's defensive avoidance disguised as self-protection.

5. You pull away when things get real

They open up. You change the subject. Or ghost them. Not because you don't care—but because you don't want to mess it up, so you bail. But silence is still a message.

Wait… Are You the Asshole in This Conversation?

Here's the tricky part: you don't have to try to be an asshole to act like one. Sometimes it's the little things:

- Constantly interrupting
- Always shifting the topic back to yourself
- Needing to be right

If that's you, even occasionally, then congrats—you're human. But also, it's time to tighten it up.

A Simple Fix:

Let people finish their sentence. Then respond with two full things about what they just said before you change the subject. That can look like:

- Asking a question
- Reflecting back
- Adding something useful

That rhythm shows: "I'm listening. I give a shit. This isn't a monologue."

Final Note:

Yeah, yeah—you can wrestle bears, outrun explosions, and fart confidence into every room you enter. But if you can't show kindness without demanding credit for it, you're missing the point.

Chivalry isn't about grand gestures. It's about invisible choices—the stuff no one sees but everyone feels.

Gentleman Check:

- Are you listening to understand, or waiting to respond?
- Are you making people feel seen, or just tolerated?
- Are you reliable, even when no one's watching?

Final Thought:

Not every socially awkward moment is full-on asshole behavior. Sometimes, it's a guy trying to connect with duct-taped instincts and a box of half-formed habits. But if you care? If you want to show up better?

Then good news: you're not doomed. You're just overdue for an upgrade.

THE BIG TRUTH ABOUT HUMAN COMMUNICATION:

How to Say Something (And Why It's Basically a Miracle Every Time)

A breakdown for normal humans with a beating heart and a tired brain.

Step 1: You Have a Thought

But here's the catch:

You don't think in sentences. You think in feelings, half-shaped ideas, flashes of memory, weird gut reactions, maybe a little anxiety, and something your mom said in 2007 that suddenly popped up for no reason.

It's like trying to explain a dream you only remember the vibe of.

Step 2: You Try to Turn That Vibe Into Words

Your brain now has to take that blob of internal chaos and run it through a translation machine made of:

- Your vocabulary
- Your emotional state
- Your social filters
- How tired you are
- And whether you're afraid of being judged

It's like you're squeezing a thunderstorm into a tiny sandwich bag and hoping the label makes sense.

Step 3: Your Mouth Tries to Cooperate

Now your body jumps in—your tongue, your breath, your vocal cords, your jaw—all trying to form words in the right tone, volume, and rhythm.

Meanwhile, your brain is like:

"Make sure they don't think I'm mad. Or needy. Or passive aggressive. Or flirting. Or dumb. Just be chill. But expressive. But casual. But articulate."

No pressure.

Step 4: Your Sound Enters Their Head

This is where things get real dicey.

Your carefully chosen sentence floats through the air…

…vibrates inside their skull…

…and gets translated again by their brain.

Only now, they add their filters:

- What mood they're in

- What baggage they're carrying
- What they think you meant
- What they're afraid you meant
- What their ex probably would've meant

Suddenly, "Did you eat the last cookie?" becomes "You don't appreciate me, do you?"

Step 5: They React

Now they send their version of your message back to you—filtered, re-translated, emotionally charged.

You get their reply and go:

"Wait, that's not what I meant at all."

And this, friends, is where misunderstandings are born.

So Why Does This Matter?

Because every time someone tries to express a feeling, a need, or even just a thought, they're running an obstacle course blindfolded.

And every time someone misunderstands you, it's not always because they're wrong—it's because there are a lot of hoops for meaning to jump through.

So here's the takeaway:

- Give people a little grace. Words are hard.
- Ask what they meant, not just what they said.
- Be proud when you communicate well—it's a full-body magic trick.
- And when it doesn't land right? Pause and say:

"That didn't come out the way I meant it. Let me try again."

Because even if we don't always say it perfectly…

The effort to be understood is one of the most beautiful things about being human.

So how do we reduce misunderstandings?

You can't eliminate them—but you can minimize distortion by mastering three things:

1. Clarity of Intent

Before you speak, ask:

What exactly am I trying to communicate—emotionally and logically?

If you know your true intent, you can guide your delivery better.

2. Emotional Framing

Match your words to your emotional state. People pick up more from how you say something than what you say.

"I'm fine"
with a smile not equal
"I'm fine"
through clenched teeth.

3. Real-time Feedback

The best communicators don't just speak—they watch how it lands.

- Did the person wince?
- Get confused?
- Pull back?
- Smile with relief?

Check in, adjust, ask: "Wait, did that come out right?" or "Let me try that again."

You're not crazy for feeling like this is infinite. It is.

But you're already doing what most don't:

You're stepping outside the automatic flow and thinking about the gears behind it.

That's rare. That's powerful.

CHAPTER 9:

THIS SHIT MATTERS

Here's the thing about chivalry—everybody talks about it like it's some dusty concept from a knight's bedtime story. You'll hear people say, "Chivalry is dead," like it's a tragic loss... but honestly, most people never understood it in the first place.

Chivalry isn't just about pulling out a chair or paying for dinner.

Chivalry originally referred to the medieval code of conduct followed by knights. It combined qualities like bravery, honor, courtesy, and a readiness to help the weak, especially in service to one's lord, country, or a lady.

Over time, the term evolved and now is often used more broadly to describe polite, respectful, and considerate behavior, especially by men toward women.

In short:

(Empathy + Respect + Integrity) Helping others = Chivalry

My educated guess? Chivalry might just be the antidote to asshole behavior.

A Knight's Code (Without the Shiny Armor)

Back in the day, knights had an actual code. It wasn't just about "Whipping out your Excalibur to slay dragons in the streets and wenches in the sheets. Or going on magical quests with some weird old dude who calls himself Merlin, handing out magic mushrooms." It was about protecting the weak, showing restraint with power, acting with honor, and serving something bigger than themselves.

Modern chivalry doesn't need chainmail. It needs presence.

You show it when:

- You keep your word, even when it costs you something.

- You offer your seat to someone not because they look frail, but because you're strong enough to stand.

- You treat the janitor and the CEO the exact same way—like human beings with dignity.

- You shut the hell up and listen when someone's trusting you with something real. Don't mistake their words as your business to share—what they told you is still theirs, not yours to spread.

Chivalry isn't performative—it's quiet power. You don't do it for applause; you do it because it's right. And trust me, people will notice—you just have to keep showing up long enough.

Real Chivalry vs. Fake Gentleman Bullshit

Jumping in to "spot" a woman at the gym just to smell her?

That's not protective—it's predatory. You're not being helpful; you're being a creep.

Paying for a date and expecting at least a hand job later?
That's not generosity—it's a transaction. You're not a gentleman; you're a vending machine with boundary issues.

Eating the last bite "As a joke"?
You think it's funny, but it tells her she's not special enough to override even your most basic of impulse controls. The joke's on you dumb shit. Good luck getting any kind of "job" after wolfing down the last of her brownies.

Chivalry is strength with self-restraint. Grace with grit. Kindness without conditions.

But What About… You Know… Women?

Ah yes, the part everyone jumps to.

Let's set this straight: chivalry isn't about women. It's about you.

You don't open doors, carry heavy bags, or walk street-side because you think women can't. You do it because it shows respect. And because you choose to lead with consideration instead of entitlement.

Chivalry has nothing to do with thinking someone is fragile. It's about showing you're not a threat, and that your strength is something you've trained to control, not impose.

Chivalry in the Wild

Want to see chivalry in action? It looks like:

- Letting someone merge in traffic even when they don't "deserve" it.

- Being the first to de-escalate when people start whipping their emotions around.

- Walking your drunk friend home, noticed he shit himself, and never mentioning it again

- Offering help without waiting for credit

No spotlight. No hashtag. No need to prove it.

Chivalry Isn't Dead. But It Is Rare.

It's rare because it's hard.

It means swallowing your ego when you're either right or wrong.

It means showing strength in how you protect—not how you control.

It means being kind to people who'll never pay you back.

But here's the deal: a gentleman doesn't do it because it's easy. He does it because connection dies without it.

Gentleman Check:

- Do you hold doors for people only when they're attractive?

- Do you offer help without strings—or do you keep receipts?
- Are you leading with your values—or waiting for someone else to go first?

Now look—I get it. Maybe you don't give a shit about knights. That's fine. But if you think they were soft, let me introduce you to a different kind of badass: the Stoic.

You know what's more impressive than winning an argument? Having such self-control, you avoid it in the first place. Stoicism isn't about being cold or emotionless—it's about choosing how you respond when life (or people) tests your patience, pride, or self-worth.

If Chivalry is the way you treat others, Stoicism is how you manage yourself.

What Stoicism Actually Is (Not the Meme Version)

Forget the YouTube pill color crap. Real Stoicism isn't about flexing your jawline in the mirror—it's about building an inner fortress. It's the ancient philosophy of choosing reason over reaction, values over emotions, and long-term peace over short-term validation.

The four virtues of Stoicism:

1. Wisdom–Think before you act. Learn before you speak.
2. Courage–Do the right thing even when it's hard.
3. Justice–Treat others fairly, even when they don't deserve it.
4. Temperance–Self-control. Don't let your feelings drive the bus.

Sound familiar? Yeah. It's basically a blueprint for not being an asshole.

Everyday Stoic Moves (aka How to Shut Up, Breathe, and Not Flip Out)

- Someone cuts you off in traffic?
  You don't control them. You do control whether you scream into the windshield like a feral raccoon.

- Your coworker takes credit for your idea?
  You don't control them. You control whether you go full passive-aggressive or scream so hard you bust a few blood vessels. Let some of it go! Handle it like a grown-up. Weigh whether it's worth the emotional energy. Being seen as the person who handles things with confidence and class often goes further than being the person who "wins" every credit dispute.

- Someone disrespects you in front of others?

    You don't control them. You control whether you escalate the disrespect—or show you're bigger than the moment. The trick isn't about "winning" the moment—it's about not letting it own you.

When it happens, especially with an audience, your ego will beg you to clap back, to make it even, to drop the verbal hammer. But what actually makes you look stronger? Not taking it personally.

Even if people laugh. Even if it stings.

You can laugh it off like it was a weak attempt at humor—

You don't have to swing back harder.

Gentleman Check:

Are you trying to win the room—or own the moment without losing yourself?

What Stoicism Isn't

- It's not emotional suppression.
  It's feeling the emotion and still choosing a response that aligns with who you want to be.

- It's not apathy.
  You still care—you just don't let the chaos control your choices.

- It's not about looking calm to seem cool.
  It's about being calm because you've trained your character.

Here's a hot take:

The ability to balance your emotions, actions, and decisions in a way that reflects responsibility, self-control, and respect for others.

Some key parts of it:

- **Self-awareness**→ You know your strengths, flaws, and impulses—and don't let them run the show.

- **Accountability**→ You own your choices, good or bad, instead of shifting blame.

- **Patience**→ You can delay instant gratification for something better down the line.

- **Empathy**→ You recognize how your words and actions affect other people.

- **Consistency**→ You don't change your standards depending on who's watching.

At its core, maturity isn't about age—it's about how you show up in the world.

Social Evolution: From Caveman to Gentleman

A caveman grunts, throws a bone, and picks fights over everything.

An evolved man knows what and when their words will have the most impact, when to shut up, and when to walk away with his dignity (and possibly his relationship) intact.

Being a mature human means understanding that not everything deserves your energy, and not every moment is about you. It's about delayed reactions, better boundaries, and choosing peace over petty victories.

Funny but True Signs You're Becoming Mature:

- You hear drama and physically feel your soul stepping back.

- You don't argue with drunk people or internet strangers.

- You see red flags and don't try to turn them into beach towels.

- You start replying with "Got it," instead of an entire paragraph.

- You value your peace more than being right.

- You're no longer the loudest guy in the room—but somehow still the one people look to.

Being the Eye of the Storm

(Look—people are going to be dramatic. They're going to gossip, stir shit, and show up acting like you're their therapist with a six-pack. Let them spin.

Your job?

Stay rooted. Listen without judging or trying to fix anything. Stay unshakable.
Let the immature guy's chase chaos like it's a Tinder match. You're past that. You've evolved.)

CHAPTER 10:

NOBODY'S PERFECT

At the end of the day, it's about being someone people don't dread seeing walk into a room. They will be far more interested in speaking with you when they understand you do genuinely care about building great friendships.

You're going to mess up. You're going to snap, overshare, under listen, or quote a YouTube guy with way too many protein tubs behind him.

It happens.

But if you can:

- Learn from it,
- Own it,
- Apologize like an adult,
- And adjust without turning it into a TED Talk.
- Then you're already ahead of most people.

Gentleman Check:

Are you walking away from this book with better habits—or just better insults?

It's ridiculous to expect anyone to master all of this.

To be reasonable just pick one—and pin that shit to the floor. **Full send.**

Lock in on Empathy, Accountability, Connection, Ownership, Growth, Honesty, Understanding, Openness, or Contribution.

Whichever one you pick, laser-focus on it until people start noticing something's different about you—and they won't even know what.

That's how you start changing your world without announcing it.
That's how you stop being that guy.

Final Gentleman Check:

You don't need to be perfect. Simply stop doing asshole things.

Whether you bought this book, borrowed it, stole it from your buddy's bathroom (Which honestly fits) or if this was hurled at your face? Just try and keep in mind. The world doesn't need more perfect people. It needs more people who embrace the main theme of this entire book.

> # Just don't be an asshole.

Made in the USA
Coppell, TX
20 January 2026

THE GENTLEMAN'S PLAYBOOK

ACTIVE INGREDIENT: Effort

USE: Take twice a month until improvement kicks in. After that, a yearly booster keeps the ego in check.

WARNINGS
- Butterflies in the belly and sudden cold self-realization may occur.
- Within the first few weeks, you may experience the uncomfortable sensation of people actually having your back — not just being at your back. This is normal.
- Temporary dizziness from realizing you were the problem that one time is normal.
- If you begin treating others better without being asked... breathe. It's just maturity.

SIDE EFFECTS
- Boosted emotional intelligence
- Reduced asshole tendencies
- Ability to apologize without spiraling
- Doors mysteriously begin opening for others

Congrats — you're leveling up.